D1094241

SONNETS
TO AN
IMAGINARY
MADONNA

BY VARDIS FISHER

OPAL LAUREL HOLMES

PUBLISHER

ISBN 0-918522-60-9

"Monogamic societies present a decent visage and a hideous rear."
—*George Meredith.*

"After the illumination, when the lovelamp is put out . . . and by the common daylight we look at the picture, what a daub it looks!"
—*Thackeray.*

"If it were not for the practical difficulties attending it, virtue would hardly be distinguishable from a kind of sensuality."
—*Bishop Wilson.*

I do not quite agree with Schopenhauer
That woman's only function is as bride;
Nor yet with those who unctuously confide
That syphilis it was that turned him sour.
I do not think that he, with all his dower
Of mad perversity, set out to ride
The race into oblivious suicide
Because he found a bee within a flower.

I do not, most emphatically; and yet
There are such women as would put a man
In love with any vile and sinful plan
To send them hellward, and make him forget
That though the bees sting he will leave his star
And come back down to seek where flowers are!

I

Madonna mistress, I have waited long
For some wild lovely Sappho who would thwart
The God of hatred and usurp my heart;
For one alive with dance and full of song
To shut away forever in eclipse
This shrouded loneliness, and bid me play
The man to artful vanities that lay
Their little ecstasies upon his lips.

And now that you have come, from God knows
                              where,
And now that you will vanish, God knows
                              when,
Shall I not multiply by eight or ten
Your virtues, and so leave you unaware?
Enthrone you far and high like some divinity
Frigidly perishing in her virginity?

1

II

Or take you as all men take women whom
They swear to love till death? Alas, too late
It is to promise that, for God or fate,
Or other recreant conniving doom
Too soon annuls the marriage oath of groom;
And to the bride of perjury and hate
It gives a woman's patience to await
The years that turn her heart into a tomb.

You know not what large losses and what gains
Unfaithfulness and faithfulness allow;
What ruthless methods Nature's are, and how
She builds one's pleasures from another's pains;
Nor by what countless ways, through what rose
                    lanes
She shows a man the folly of his vow.

III

Of all the people you have known has one
Gone from the altar and his way in peace?
Who has not sought or wished for his release,
And dreamed of new trails, though he followed
none?
Among the millions spinning round the sun
Have you not seen what every mortal sees:
That men who mate, like migratory geese,
May sever like them ere the year is done?

And if they do not part, as, I admit,
Is oftentimes the case, no one can say
That either good or ill will come of it,
Or that the gander should have flown away;
Although some may surmise that those who fly
Do often find the altitude too high.

IV

But, my Madonna, do not think that I,
Because my eyes have seen a thing or two,
Hold women in contempt or fear that you
Will ever bring to me a wish to fly.
Like any other, we've a mind to try
The way of love, and if we find too few
The pleasures, we shall do what we must do
And leave to higher power the reason why.

Whate'er we do there's nothing much at all
For any sage or fool to wonder at.
We're only puppets, fanning at the bat,
Or phantoms fighting, backs against the wall;
Or if excuse must stronger be than that,
There's always Eve's disgrace and Adam's fall.

V

Oh, I shall take your virtues lean and slender
And magnify them to such queenly sizes
That you will seem a wondrous thing and
                                    tender,
Hiding in strange ineffable surprises.
And of your little soulless inept vanities
Your male Penelope will weave distortions,
Till eyes bewildered by your new proportions
Will find a wonder in your least inanities.

Then in the gorgeous myth of my romancing
You'll be expropriated of your vices;
And truth to love will make its sacrifices
The while I seek for delicate enhancing
New flatteries, until without half trying
You will believe me when you know I'm lying!

And if my faith is small I trust that pride
Will compensate, and draw the stubborn eyes
From other women who may advertise
Whatever qualities you lack as bride.
I trust that disillusionment will guide
To safe respectability, and rise
In decent attitudes when I devise
Excuses for the things I cannot hide.

The way of faithfulness, my love, believe me,
Is a long lane of roses and more roses;
And I could never utterly deceive thee,
Unless in ways by which the heart proposes
That nothing can be faithless or deplorable
Except the things which make you less adorable!

Nor shall there come a moment soon or ever
When I shall wish to make minute correction
Or any minor flaw in you, or fancy
That any power short of necromancy
Conceived and executed one whose graces
Are lovelinesses made of commonplaces;
Nor fail to thank the Lord for His endeavor
That crowned one effort with your smooth
                                    perfection.

I'll yield asceticism to my duty,
And if I find your lips too eager, surely
I shall not love less deeply or less purely;
For if you are too amorous for beauty,
I shall be forced to think that in Nirvana
There is much more of Eve than of Diana.

VIII

Sometimes when the emasculated scheme
Of heaven or of hell (that made of mud
A baffled phantom housed in flesh and blood,
A dark futility clothed with a dream):
When its dull impotence is then arrayed
In passion avid as a naked fire,
We shall yield sensitiveness to desire,
And shudder as souls shudder when betrayed.

And after disgust rejuvenates our wits
And dignity assumes its former sway,
You'll be as unapproachable as Cato;
And I, convulsed by all your counterfeits
Of culture and of decency, will say:
Madonna, do you now believe in Plato?

IX

Oh we shall talk of love in all the tongues
With which all mortal lovers strive to measure
The subtle intonations of their pleasure;
And we shall climb intrepidly the rungs
Of passion's ladder till a perfect bliss
Of blue and stars will open like a story
Of fairyland and moonlight, and a kiss
Will lift our glory high to heaven's glory.

And after we exhaust the artless ways
That hold the mirror of your heart to mine,
We still shall seek a more convincing sign
Of love and of its endlessness of days;
And with the night's confession fresh above you,
You'll ask: You love me? and I'll say: I love you.

X

In lovers' parlance there's a euphemistic
Term for lust: they call it honeymoon;
And usually they pitch it into June
Where it is both retiring and sadistic.
And courtship, that was flatulently cystic
Of pent emotions, breaks into a croon
Of Nature's ancient language, till the tune
At last grows most indubitably atavistic.

Madonna, will our vivid consummation
Of heaven's plan bring us what it has brought
All those whom marriage licensed to explore?
Some thirty days of hectic exploration,
The moon as changeless as it was before,
The honey eaten, and an empty pot?

I saw two honeymooners, wonder-eyed,
Exploring what home training and the church,
Religion's gyves and the parental birch
And forty other taboos had denied.
I heard them gurgle cooingly and chide
Like mating blackbirds clinging to a perch,
As eyes were busy in the eager search
For what was bridegroom and for what was
                        bride.

And so while Nature fawned indulgently,
They gave their full attention to her plan.
They doubtless thought they loved and dreamed
                        a bit
Of what eternal bliss would come of it;
And Nature smiled and knew that it would be
Another woman or another man.

XII

This will not do, Madonna: let us speak
Of love, if speak we must, as lovers should.
It is the cynic's price on maidenhood
That measures honeymoons by day or week.
It is no lover who, with tongue in cheek,
Holds up to truth the virtuous and good;
And who would not take, when or how he
                    could,
The path where none find and forever seek.

So much for that; but bear a little while
And see what there may be to win or lose;
Bring all your dreams and longings, if you choose,
And if you can, 'tis better that you smile;
For though your faith may wander in exile,
There may be something here that you can use.

XIII

Come, let us weave the patterns of our love
Into intoxications of desire,
And prove that Nature's most transcendent fire
May safely light the bosom of the dove;
Reveal the heart and all the ways thereof
To be the restive longings which aspire
Above life's disenchantments, and above
The altars set to destiny entire.

At least so shall I deify your ways
Into a holy fabric of deceiving
That I shall with a perilous unbelieving
Become infatuated; shall so praise
With brave dishonesty the day I met you
That I at last may honestly forget you.

XIV

I'll be a mighty hero in your eyes:
Some ruthless Tamburlaine in bloody coat,
Who holds a dozen kingdoms by their throat:
I'll fill your breast with flutters of surprise,
And lift it to the fullness of a breath
While I seize terror, like a lightning-lance,
And hurl it through the womb of circumstance,
Clear through the living spaces into death.

And if my shuddering dramatic pose
Sends the blood hot along your veins, then I
Shall ask for love no clearer reason why;
Though you may know what everybody knows,
And in you ghastly aftermath of wonder
See nothing bright, and marvel at the thunder.

XV

And sometimes when in weakness I would lay
My head upon your breast and ponder on
The frightful horrors of some Abaddon,
Will you then shelter me, nor draw away?
Then with your charming trust will you placate
My conscience, and believe that all is well
When phantoms of hypocrisy and hate
Stalk past like weird Acephali from hell?

Will you then step forth gloriously to redeem
My cowardice, and see a shining alp
That is my throne, and lift me as a king
From craven depths where I am perishing?
Or then abscond and take with you a dream
Of some Amadis peeling terror's scalp?

XVI

Ah well, when I am most romantic, try
To yield naïve credulity that you
May be the one whom you are measured by:
When stars let down their lances from the blue
You'll be Andromeda, and I will fly
Like Perseus to clasp your waist; and when
The west is flame my Dejanira then
Will hang her magic garment in the sky.

Be thou not skeptical, Madonna mine,
Of Nature's plan to build my life in thine!
We dare not question what must ever be,
Nor labor when the gods would have us play:
I'll be your lover, you my love, if we
Give love its glory and the heart its way.

XVII

You will go daily where the slaughtered vies
With other slaughtered for a gruesome show;
Where hams and sides of hogs hang row on row
Among the heifer's shoulders, ribs, and thighs.
And there by roasts and stews and boils and fries
Will be the ghastly liver, brain, and tongue;
And out in front, reeking of blood and dung,
Will hang the butchered hens with glassy eyes.

"I dare say that Herr Wasserman will take
The Nobel Prize." "My dear, I think he ought."
"No doubt." "And what a very facile pen
He has for subtlety!" "True, dear. Again
What power he has, what depth and reach,
       what thought!"
This, as we chew with vigor at a steak.

XVIII

If my disgust may seem too sensitive
For life where stomachs are a reservoir
Of every substance savory, and for
Assimilation that is like a sieve
That strains all things into the will to live;
And if I find revolting this dull war
In which the stronger eat the weak, and are
Made traitors to intelligence, pray give

Your love to them whose easy scruples bring
Their self-respect intact from each debauch;
For whom, like some big infant, flesh is pap,
In whose nose blood is like the smell of Scotch;
Who prate of culture over roasts, who yap
Of art while crunching at a chicken's wing.

XIX

Call me abnormal (if you will) and shout
To please your conscience, but I beg you, note:
I'll not pretend, if flesh goes down my throat,
That anything more civilized comes out.
Of stomachs I have always had a doubt,
And fancied that they build our brains by rote;
And so if they are stuffed with ram and shoat,
What wonder if the mind's a horn or snout?

You doubtless think I am grotesque, but that's
A metaphor as apt as hands to mittens;
In this world, as in any other one,
Are fallacies seductive as small kittens;
Which folk chase, less to slay them than for fun,
Like dogs forever jumping after cats.

XX

And too: there'll come the Edythes and Elaics,
The Reginalds and Roderiques and Linns,
And heaven knows how many small mosaics
Of young credulities wrapped up in skins.
And we shall aggravate the raucous dins
Of souls that come to play a while with chains;
And we shall get for our prolific pains
A progeny outwitted by our sins.

And while you praise your Lincolns,
                    Washingtons,
And queenly Marys, I shall slink in shame
That so much mediocrity should claim
The other names of other women's sons;
But you, enamored of your power to breed,
Will sow, and water with your tears the seed.

XXI

And let me now confess it, as I should:
I'm not of those whose intellects enshroud
The feeble sophistry by which the crowd
Conceive of birth as something wise and good.
I've pondered but have never understood
Why procreation makes a father proud,
Or in what way a glory has endowed
The consequent estate of motherhood.

And though you may believe that mothers get
A gift from God and honors that befit
Their sacrifice, I sometimes have surmised
That what they pay is seldom advertised;
And I have never seen a mother yet
Who did not write with blood the name of it.

XXII

And even though the gift be free, it is
Of all gifts I have known the commonest;
For what or who the giver, his bequest
Is here for any who will make it his.
Whatever things that hum or yowl or fizz
May have the sanctuary of the nest,
And of one glory fate cannot divest
The dullest fly that ever learned to whiz.

'Tis well to make our satyriasis
And nymphomania a thing of pride,
Else we should be less egoist and slide
To even lower altitudes than this;
And having lost the worship of our kind,
Be much less happy and no doubt less blind.

XXIII

For in this war called love the indaba
Among the savages of our desire
Is too much like the councils which conspire
To make our greed the magistrate of law.
Until we stand as penitents in awe
Before our self-constructed funeral pyre
We shall go down in Babylons of fire,
Amidst the smoke of burning fang and claw.

This is an era when the heart is wet
With what the hand has killed; when people
                                        strive
To make of love a way to keep alive:
We may find love some day when we forget
Our barbarism, after we have slain
Our lust for blood and holocausts of pain.

XXIV

Sometimes, Madonna, I may think your breath
Too sweetly pure of Erebus, you know;
May wish that you'd less beautifully grow,
And choose for love a devil's shibboleth
That taunts such beauty as must rot in death;
And loving you the less for being so,
I may wish for a Ninon de l'Enclos,
A Madame Blavatsky, or a Lady Macbeth.

Will you then lay aside your angel's guise
Of innocence, and let your lover see
How wicked and how lovely you can be?
Or will you pout demurely in surprise,
And strive to be what every poet's verse
Would make you—or perhaps a little worse.

XXV

For if you do, I may grow ghastly white
With virtue if some truant Azrael
Wanders abreast of vengeance in the night
When passion holds a torch for us to hell.
And I, anæmic of a long eclipse
Of pleasure, and too weary of the drouth,
Shall flee through some red dawn and sink my
                              lips
Into some wild and luscious crimson mouth.

But after, when I've drunk me aching through
With ecstasy till each bewildered sense
Shrinks white in nausea and impotence,
My goddess, I shall feel a poignant duty
To Azrael whose virtue is in you
Impeccable and unimpassioned beauty!

XXVI

Or if I love you à la Ethel Dell
And burn this "lightning fluid" of my veins
Upon your lips; and if, alas, to well
I give love pasture and cut loose the reins;
If love is such as rends you half apart
And sets your blood on fire, will you not grant
That I am love's superb hierophant,
And Satan's finest master of its art?

No doubt! And though I conquer that and this
In you with hot ferocities that kiss
Your breath away, I shall not cease to gape
With wonder, as I seize you by the hair,
That things which are so lovely and so fair
Can swoon to ecstasy against the ape!

XXVII

There is a virgin whom some men call love:
We ravish her and learn how thin the ice
Of virtue which convention froze above
A depth that has an undertow of vice.
And why, of all things mortal, does she shun
The lighted streets?—and too, why does she
                flaunt
An angel's face the while her kisses haunt
A man till he is naked and undone?

I do not know, Madonna, but I think
That you had better keep your angel's guise.
I want to think that love is love, because
In novels it is not all fangs and claws;
So hide me from the devil in your eyes,
Else I shall leave you quicker than a wink.

XXVIII

Love's tome is weighty and somewhat aghast
At leaves whose edges have been burnt by
                              flames,
And at the futile paradox that shames
The present creed with ashes of the last.
We grope a moment baffled ere we cast
Our vote with Plato or with William James;
And yet in death, one name for all our names,
For all, the acid chaos of the past.

What folly that in love we go posthaste
Along a million lanes, when all turn back
And join ere death to make a single track!
And so what wrong, Madonna, in a tryst
Upon the highway, seeking lips unkissed,
Or arms sometimes about another's waist?

XXIX

I have a rather mild diathesis
That predisposes me, I fear, to spleen;
And some no doubt will think I overween,
Or that romance for me has been remiss.
And they may say that some prepotent this,
Or too ironic that has come between
My lips and the intoxicate poteen
That lovers gather from the lover's kiss.

It is not so, Madonna: pray believe
That though I may be just a trifle sour,
I am inclined to blame the lovely flower,
And not the curiosity of Eve;
And though a little timid of the bees,
I fancy there's a way to conquer these.

XXX

But let men guess, if guessing is their need.
For those who gossip most are those no doubt
Whose past, if one could turn it inside out,
Would be a womb in which repressions breed.
Theirs is an unfulfillment that would plead
For knowledge of what others are about,
And all their curiosities that sprout
From morbid wishes but betray their seed.

In this mad world so few have strength to win
Emancipation from the habits which
Abjure the unfamiliar as a sin,
And keep the conscience scurvy with an itch
To find one poisoned who somehow got stung
At flowers which they too would search among.

XXXI

We must not ogle the forbidden tree,
Nor wonder why omniscience put it there,
For those most indolently unaware
Are those whom joy accoutres cap-a-pie.
We shall be happy if we learn to be
As foolish as the happy anywhere;
And life will be both beautiful and fair
If we see only what the happy see.

There once was one in Eden who aspired
To knowledge, and it was the death of her;
She won the hell to which we have retired,
And lost her heaven; from which I infer:
It is no part of wisdom to be wise
When wisdom is no part of paradise.

XXXII

Your soul's index of sweet adagios,
And small harmonics of its violin
Will play the minor orchestrations in
Love's harmony, and only half of those.
With quiet drama and a quiet pose
You may seduce your fretful paladin
With rôles alluringly too feminine
To moods domestically quite comatose.

But when God's opera of flame and storm
Hangs its black drapery and hurls its tragic
Lightning-music through a night of magic,
I shall forget your small soprano charm,
And plunge into the night to follow after
The quivering white veins and the sky's dark
                laughter.

XXXIII

Do not call me your poet, for, God wot,
The poets of love must never dare to be
Emancipated intellectually
From moral platitudes and tommyrot.
They must sing out with fever tongues and hot
High temperatures that each of us is free,
And that each life is but an argosy
Of love—although they know that it is not.

Were I to try, I might seduce your fears;
With moral attitudinizings shoo
Away the intellectual bugaboo;
Or imitate, if you will lend your ears,
The lyrists and the lapdog sonneteers
Of man's morality. Well, here are two:

XXXIV

Come, let us run with laughter up the hill
And catch the sunlight where it first comes
                                    down;
The earth now wears the morning like a crown,
Set with the sweet gold of the daffodil.
O love, my love, come let us go and fill
Our hearts with red rose fragrance and with
                                    flame,
And we shall know the glory and the name
Of what hope conquers and death cannot kill.

For when the springtime has a flower-birth
To grow its colorul and fragrant hair,
We know what unreflective rapture there
Must be within the bosom of the earth;
And what deep ecstasy must sail the wing
Of love against the zenith of the spring!

XXXV

When wearied by the struggles which assail
A too reluctant soul that gropes in doubt,
I look at fellow beings roundabout
Betrayed by patience and with anguish pale;
And when I see what virtues often fail,
And what mischance puts honesty to rout,
While evil with a loud triumphant shout
Is throned, and all the tribes of hell prevail:

I think of you, belovèd, and the dear
Sweet beauty that is ever in your eyes,
As if some shining vision of the skies
Had left a light there; and I know that here
Where there is one so lovely and so pure,
The right will triumph and its god endure!

XXXVI

The last may copy Shakspere and the first
No one at all—but what does either prove?—
Except that when the ego falls in love
Its asininity is at its worst.
Its reason may be baffled or coerced
Until it coos like any turtledove,
And sees the bowl of heaven tipped above
Its lips, and pleasures brimming to its thirst.

And thus enamored of a huge mirage
Of optical illusions, it may cry
A while, like any babe, and by and by
Escape to the routine of its ménage;
And get a mistress or a howling brat
For disillusionment to wonder at.

XXXVII

This is not love, Madonna, any more
Than fame is glory, or theology
Religion; and it is our poetry—
Or what usurps the name—that keeps a store
Of misconceptions which our wits deplore;
As if, afraid to venture on the sea,
We sang the diapason of the free
While building toy boats upon the shore.

For love, if it will be as glad and strong
As life, must build of more heroic stuff
Than these thin sophistries; and it must slough
Its attitudes of unreflective song:
Must stud its temple with the spikes of pain,
And keep a window open to the rain.

XXXVIII

Now let me tell the fable of a bird
Who sat all day asleep upon a limb,
And who, when night put out its stars at him,
Honked louder than the loudest you have heard.
And many thought his dismal cry demurred
At brewing storms, and others called it whim
Of one who strove, because his eyes were dim,
To mock with God's expropriated third.

But be it what it will, the fact remains
That every night, yearlong, he hid from view
And tooted dolefully; and though a few
Surmised that there was madness in his veins,
Among the vast majority there grew
Belief in him as prophet of the rains.

XXXIX

Until one summer, with an owl's uncouth
Loud prescience in the destiny of storms,
He quite regaled himself on noise while farms
Grew ghastly in the aura of a drouth.
And day by day additional alarms
Played some ironic havoc with his truth,
While lava sunlight shimmered from the south,
And gnats spun upward in bewildered swarms.

And then one night the bird was heard no more,
And more weeks went before the thunder came.
A lurid avalanche of cloud and flame
Left things too wet that were too dry before;
And some who went with shotguns on a search
Found the mad prophet drowned upon his perch.

XL

My soul has no 'invincible surmise,'
Madonna mine, nor does it think its wit
Is such a compass as divides the skies
Into the parts where gods and devils sit.
Above, it sees a universe unlit
With any purpose visible to eyes;
And down below, the wing of time that flies
But graveward, drawing darkness after it.

I have no faith except in beauty, nor
A Santayana's vision in my soul;
I apprehend most clearly what things are
Only when April steps into her rôle:
Keep thou thy loveliness and I will sing
Of immortality and heaven's king!

XLI

There is in me no wisdom where all things
Are ruins shut behind a silent door;
Of what one builds when prodigal youth sings,
And naught remains of what was sung before.
There is in me no flutter of wild wings,
No Viking with an arm bent to the oar:
Only a cry to far-off vanishings,
And dust that piles around me on the floor.

Yet I among the shadows now will purr
My smooth convincing lovely chastened lies,
And feed the hunger which your lips confess;
With artful aubterfuges I will blur
Your doubting stare till your bewildered eyes
Will find a glory in my nothingness!

XLII

As you see, I am not the kind who make
The eager lover, having gone too far
From error to be what most lovers are.
I do not fancy I am such as wake
A passion in another's heart, or take
The sole possessorship and thus debar
All better men from this particular
Imprisoned one who flutters for my sake.

And if I have—'tis probable I may—
A wish to own one woman as a man
Might own a horse, and so embrace the clan
Of those who preach monogamy and play
In many houses, there may somehow be
Some other hindrances. Well, let us see.

XLIII

I will not be recruited to the squads
Who post o'er land and ocean without rest,
Nor yet to those who with a martyr's zest
Upbear the mild yoke of life's racks and rods.
I care no groatworth for the man who plods
With weary holiness, till all-obsessed
With post-death glory he abjures the best
Of life to be the puppet of his gods.

I've no clown's cargo of audacity,
No fool's presumption that would have me strive
To keep myself eternally alive;
Nor have I arrogance to wish to be
Rejuvenated from the dust, apart
From all life flowing through a common heart.

XLIV

My penury of hope does not suffice
For trust in what no eye has ever seen;
And virtue is so blasphemously lean
That I should starve to death in paradise.
I've thought of heaven only once or twice
And wondered what its orgies may have been;
And of its golden candle-sticks and queen,
And of its ruler, never more than thrice.

Nor has a fretful apathy of life
Betrayed me to a wish to watch with God
When all the bloodless phantoms from the sod
Rise up to be forever free of strife:
I'd rather have the darkness and the doubt
Than be a ghost when all the stars are out.

XLV

I know some are, Madonna, who will yowl
At what I say and call my words obscene;
Who will assert that it is bitter spleen
That has perverted me to something foul.
And some—the ones who deified the owl—
Will strut about their sacrosanct demesne,
And think that heaven's otiose routine
Has given holy sanction to their howl.

I shall not hear them and you must ignore,
For God has made some very noisy clay;
And after all they have no more to say
Than what has been said many times before;
There are some hypocrites alive today,
And in the grave there are a million more.

XLVI

There never has been one who dared to tell
How perjured truth becomes the moral code,
Who did not find his back against the goad
Of cowardice, and hear the pious yell.
And he who dares to storm the citadel
Of righteousness until its lies explode
Will find himself acclaimed the vilest toad
That ever missed the bottom of the well.

It does not matter, really, and the saints
For all their cry may be as pure as sinners;
We all of us are only small beginners
In virtue and its nimbus of restraints;
And though some think and others make
                        complaints,
It's doubtful whether any will be winners.

XLVII

The pious and the impious both frown
Upon the other's way of life, and stir
Their wits to make them seem as vile as were
Those ancients ere Jehovah bade them drown.
And though they win ephemeral renown
As piety's or as evil's pensioner,
They are with zeal the same chronologer
Of all the errors not yet written down.

And we, no less; so let us now adjust
Our purpose more serenely to the sum
Of what we shall be when the end has come:
A giant's handful of forgotten dust
To which time will consign, because it must,
The empire and the hope of Christendom.

XLVIII

It is the optimism of the fool
That mouths such words as only hope can spell,
And struts triumphant with its bagatelle
Of faith that dares not put itself to school.
Its votaries who spurn truth's ridicule
May prove by apathy that all is well,
As things are always proved when fear of hell
Makes common sense half-brother to the mule.

It is an easy way by which we blink
Our duty here and reap the profit there.
So very few, there are, who dare to drink
The cup of pain apportioned as their share;
And there is none who ever learns to think
Until he finds the bedrock of despair.

XLIX

Do not expect, Madonna, any brave
Emasculated righteousness from me;
I've learned how little difference may be
Between the matin-chanter and the knave.
And I have heard the theologian rave
Of legends that have raped credulity,
But all this talk of purpose brings to me
The futile clamor leading to the grave.

To blaring bands we march like blinded men
Up from the shadows to disordered lives;
And having killed a fox or traded wives,
We're off upon the endless march again;
And so we come and go and go and come,
With God and all His devils at the drum.

L

And am I cynic if I sometimes say
What God expunged when all the devils fled?
There is no wisdom in the wisest head,
Nor sin if some laugh while the others pray.
For those who claim to know are only they
Who claim to read what none has ever read;
And after everything is done and said
We see no more than we saw yesterday.

We cannot know what things we look upon,
Nor what may come next where the morning
                                   came.
There may be chaos dogging out the dawn,
And only void behind a sunset flame;
Or there behind the beauty of the clouds
May be the dead, descending in their shrouds.

LI

I know that you may turn a quiet ear
To listen to some ego's platitudes;
When sophistry inebriates your moods,
You may believe that there are things to hear.
And jaundiced by both prejudice and fear
You may give credence to religious feuds,
And fancy that some *ism* and its broods
Have cleared what all of time may never clear.

But you will learn, if apt, that all the roar
And tumult of our life amounts to this:
Some slay the phantoms of their cowardice,
And some there are who leave them as before;
And while one chases ghosts that he has laid,
The other brays above the cannonade.

LII

I hope therefore that you will give no heed
To unproductive vagaries that men
Have called philosophies, and may again.
Of universal knowledge they can read
A line or two perhaps and make a creed;
But their prolific orgies of the pen
Are like the frantic cackling of a hen
The votaries of an antiquated need.

Else you, like many others who have sung
The many chambers of what they have built,
Will stab yourself with error to the hilt;
And will at each disturbing noise among
The dim self-conjured specters of your house
Pursue a phantom and forget the mouse.

LIII

Madonna, it is impotence that sends
Us to our metaphysics for a goal.
We play, because we must, a senseless rôle
That holds no guarantee of dividends.
And whether we make enemies or friends,
And whether death is but an empty hole,
Our purpose still is futile, and our soul
A supererogation of our ends.

We're sure of this—if we know anything:
That purpose as conceived by mortal mind
Is like a bird that darkness has made blind,
Climbing the sky upon an aimless wing;
For in a mirror showing time and place
Would be no image of the human face.

LIV

That time is dead, I fear, for any man
Whose ego does not hold his brain in thrall,
For we can see that to a waterfall
The stray drops come as swiftly as they can.
We are like water, boiling in a pan,
Whose drops rise on strange errands to a wall,
And cling a moment and a moment fall
To seek the level from which they began.

For though in our distress we may cut loose
From everything an hour or two, and stain
A spot of life with liberated pain,
After we reach the headgate of our sluice
We shall flow back into the pan again,
And learn that boiling is of little use.

LV

This life, Madonna, is a juggernaut
With sightless eyes and blood upon its hand;
Its brain as purposeless as flying sand,
Or vapor rising from a boiling pot.
And what at last may be its destined lot,
By whom conceived or by what power planned
Will find no answer till we understand
Why roses bloom a day and fall and rot.

It matters not what wisdom or what wit,
Or other hopeless folly of the mind
May set a shining goal for humankind,
And prove its fallacy by holy writ;
We only know that blind we come, and blind
We go where blindness is the end of it.

LVI

It is not, pray believe me, that I doubt
That good is good or that a sin is sin;
Or that the gods were all Olympian
Until they caught mortality and gout.
Nor has it ever been my way to flout
The fight that we are losing and may win,
And I still hope that there is purpose in
The universe, or somewhere roundabout.

Nor do I doubt that diligent endeavor
Can make a heaven of our pantomime,
Or that evangelism is a lever
To pry away the incubus of crime;
Or that if you and I should live forever
Our love would smoothly synchronize with time!

LVII

I have loved life and love it, but I know
How ruthless it can be with those too weak
To find unerringly the path they seek,
And give adversity a blow for blow.
And I have seen the strong as blindly go
As any where the grimmest struggles wreak
Their pitiless passion till the wretched meek
Yield cravenly before an unseen foe.

Yes, I love life, but I do not devise
A veil to hide what faith cannot redeem.
I'd rather rise in anger and blaspheme
The ugly part of it than moralize
As millions do, whose small myopic eyes
Peer out from some preadolescent dream.

LVIII

You must walk fearlessly and straight ahead
If you would go with me, for I have been
Too long delayed by those who stop to win
A heaven and who find a hell instead.
You must abjure the sentimental dread
Of those who fence off righteousness from sin;
Nor must you ever look behind to spin
A halo from the ashes of the dead.

And unbelievers though we be, we'll go
Into the grave with unreluctant feet;
And leaving all the bitterness, the sweet,
We'll step into death's quiet undertow,
And trust that all the racket underground
Will not awake us when the trumpets sound.

LIX

But here we are and somehow should be glad
Because we can be very sure of that.
We may not be much wiser than the bat,
And not one half as happy as the shad.
And yet there is no reason to be sad,
What though our hopes may be a trifle flat,
For we've more baffling things to wonder at
Than any our forefathers ever had.

These are the interests that keep all men
From setting out to suicide en masse;
The glory and the mystery would pass
If words set down by any mortal's pen
Showed wide highways to God; and I, alas,
Would lose them all that I might seek again!

LX

Such is the scanty little I believe,
And 'tis not, as you must have clearly seen,
The sort of thing that keeps the myrtle green.
Nor does it labor bravely to retrieve
The sad misfortune of the sinful Eve.
It is not even, as it might have been
From many other pens, a rosy lien
On heaven, or from hell a brief reprieve.

But in its way, I trust, it has deplored
Our tragic waste of effort and the kink
In every destiny; nor does it shrink
From what its feeble vision can afford
Of truth; nor will it hesitate to wink
At death when it shall feel the naked sword.

LXI

I cannot say what moods will not retrieve me
From this infatuation with your graces,
Or what unhappy longings will deceive me
To promises of love on other faces.
I dare say that somewhere in open spaces
Of other hearts some unpossessed emotions
May shake me deeply as the storms the oceans,
And show white sails in strange and far-off
                                    places.

But I shall be as faithful as the bees are,
And everything that draws its life to beauty;
Nor dare to let an artificial duty
Hide from my eyes what Nature's stern decrees
                                    are;
And you will be both lark and rose as long
As you are lovelier than flowers and song.

61

LXII

It may be you will love the smooth domains
Of daylight where no meteors are streaming;
I darkness, where the farthest stars are gleaming
Like candles set by heaven's window-panes.
You may prefer the old and soft refrains,
And I the tumult and the raucous screaming;
It may be you will love an April's dreaming,
And I its wild winds running through the rains.

And yet what quiet or what frenzied thing
May draw us deeply and may draw us far,
Ever for me will all the voices sing
Of the wild melody of what you are;
And here or yonder, on the earth or skies,
You'll find a devil in your paradise.

LXIII

And if this continuity of madness
Called birth and death may round my cycle ere
                                        you
Have reached your noon, my parting will
                              endear you
To one small brief efficiency of sadness.
And for a summer's length you will assure me
With daily sacrifices to forgetfulness,
And turn at last, forgiving in regretfulness,
From darkness and the silence that allure me.

But God will give you mercy like a jewel,
And after years have gone you'll understand then
His secrets clearly and His deepest ways well;
And when you look upon my picture, you'll
Murmur, *O my love! my lover!*—and then:
I wonder if his eyes were blue or hazel.

LXIV

And what though you have found another one
To trade his kisses and his smiles for yours;
To do the little odd romantic chores
That keep a lover shining in the sun:
What though your charms may keep him on the
                                              run
To match his energy with what allures,
And there are half a thousand signatures
Of love appended to what he has done:

Belovèd, make whatever happy terms
You please with love, and may love bring to you
New rituals until you turn your head
Away from memories of what is dead;
For I shall be too busy with the worms
To give a moment's heed to what you do.

LXV

How like a willow are you now when at
A gesture or a word you spring alert;
But when I see, as once, the full inert
Deposit of your mother where she sat;
And when the sprawled circumference of that
Comes back to mind, as when I saw her skirt
Precariously taut around her girt,
I shudder at the tyranny of fat.

And so will you, when thirty years have gone
And hung their refuse to your waist and hips,
Sink deep into what time has battened on;
And she whom love chose for her slenderness
Will writhe within her prodigal excess,
And choke with pain when youth is at her lips.

LXVI

And I may wearily grow deathly sick
Of futile breasts that sag, and of the night
That grows in eyes that once were shining light;
Of skin that once was lovely growing thick
And wrinkled to the mouth: too much of this
Will make of love a frightful ugly thing:
A horror waiting on a trembling wing,
A loathing breaking from its chrysalis.

The years triumphantly will call us liar
And turn our love to pasture on a grin
Stuck like a pallor from our brow to chin.
Rather than this, let us now heap desire
From heart to brimming lip and perish in
A kiss of flame, an ecstasy of fire!

LXVII

What dark things shining are your eyes when sex
Holds thee in thrall! I marvel much to know
How it can light your eyes with wonder so.
And strange that love so rapturous can vex
My heart with coldness; strange that when you
                                    sit
With breast against my heart and lips to mouth,
I draw into the shelter of my drouth
And peer out at your light and ponder it!

I wonder: can it be that I may fear
What may come after love is done with us?
May it not be a spirit's shrinking thus
From pleasures that betray us? O my dear,
Were it not wiser much to beggar this
And keep lips hungry for your lips to kiss!

LXVIII

To us somewhere and time will come a day
When we shall falter where we dared to run,
And seeing that our backs are to the sun,
We shall look round to find another way.
We shall have danced the fretful roundelay,
And found the working and the playing done;
And with no more that may be lost or won,
Sit down to say what there remains to say.

Then through a mist we shall look back upon
The footprints turning blindly down the years;
And from the paths the morning will be gone,
And grey dust heaped on unremembered biers;
When silence sleeps in love's forgotten themes,
And ashes blur the patterns of our dreams.

LXIX

That hour will come when we shall look across
The gulf that time will build between us two,
And in the rainbow bridge from me to you
Appraise the perjured colors and the loss.
And while we contemplate the gold and dross
Of what we've done and what we have to do,
We'll march the years in saturnine review
To learn if God or Satan won the toss.

And if God loses and if Satan wins,
And if a devil throws a loaded dice,
We need not wonder why the rainbows are
So substanceless and evanescent, for
No doubt the gulf between will quite suffice
To be a sepulchre of all our sins.

LXX

The time will also come, so I am told,
When we with eyes grown used to seeing things
Will gaze at wisdom and what wisdom brings,
And salvage patience as our hearts turn cold.
And as two pageantries of death unfold,
We'll take our fingers from the broken strings,
And we to whom a shadow faintly clings
Will part at last with shadows when we're old.

And when the final moment comes to go,
Our hands will draw away, and each of us
Who were so much together will descend
Alone, below the level of the end;
And shaken by our loneliness, we'll know
Only that lovers love and vanish thus.

LXXI

And in the sad reflectiveness of age
What will be with us then of our romance
To give us fealty when the arrogance
Of our regrets has come upon the stage?
What will abide with lovers to assuage
The brooding heart when in the countenance
Of unremembered love it sees mischance
Alone of all that gave it tutelage?

Ah, in that time when hearts, no matter how,
Look back upon the paths by which they came,
They bring to light what formerly in blame
They hid from conscience; and the perjured vow
That you and I would make so gladly now
Becomes the ugly bastard of their shame.

LXXII

Real love, O doubt not, is a golden thing
Which all of us alloy with the lead
Of our own beings. It were better dead
Than prostituted by our offering
Of flesh alone; and it were wise to sing
Of what is nearer to our hearts instead;
And then, perchance, no lover need have said
What age now counts in every reckoning.

What men call love is passion that equips
Us with irreconcilables that spin
A senseless network of deceit and sin;
And like the spider, spinning with our lips
We catch one, or occasionally there slips
A thread and we ourselves are tangled in.

LXXIII

Madonna, my Madonna, let each take
His dreams, and let us go our separate ways!
Across the unfulfilled, the empty days,
Will be a silence where no hearts will break.
There then will be no agony, no ache
Of lips unkissed, no unremembered face;
No shadows hugging round a vacant place,
No vigil in a night when phantoms wake.

Go back, and we shall keep our dreams, and
                round
Them build a garden of all loveliness,
And set wide-open gates for our egress
When love has wearied us of sight and sound;
And having these, we need not strive to see
A path for two where there is room for three.

VARDIS FISHER
WAS NOT A MORMON

In a book, **The Mormon Experience**, published in March, 1979 (Alfred A. Knopf, Inc., released by Random House), Davis Bitton and his collaborator, Leonard J. Arrington, have a paragraph on page 330, that says:

"In the field of fiction perhaps the most important writer of Mormon background has been Vardis Fisher, whose series **Tetralogy** (1932-23) and **Testament of Man** (1947-1960) are recognized as major achievements. There are differences of opinion on Fisher's importance, perhaps, and it may be that the next generation will be in a better position to evaluate him. In any case, his Mormon upbringing had a powerful influence not only on Children of God (1939), a novelistic, basically sympathetic retelling of the Mormon epic, but also on his other novels."

THIS IS A LIE. Arrington knew that it was a lie; but it is possible that Bitton did not. Arrington knew that although Fisher's parents had been baptized into the Mormon Church as children, they did not practice the faith; and cared so little about Mormonism, that they never bothered to have their own children baptized. Mormon influence was negligible during Fisher's formative years, almost non-existant. The strong religious influence in his life — strong to the brink of disaster — was the **Old Testament**, as Leonard Arrington well knows.

But at the age of twenty (1915), Vardis was voluntarily baptized into the Mormon Church, because, like so many young people today, he needed an anchor for his life, and hoped to find it in this religious cult. However, when he read the Mormon literature after his baptism, he was appalled to learn what the Mormons really believe, and left the Church immediately — within the year — an apostate, without ever having experienced a religious conversion. There was no Mormon bias in his thinking, except in a negative way — his life-long hatred of the "tyranical hierarchy which exerts such rigid control over the minds and lives of the Mormons."

An even more monstrous lie than the paragraph quoted above, appears as a footnote to that paragraph, footnote 71, which cites as source material an incredibly crass piece of sophistry, by Leonard J. Arrington and Jon Haupt, which was published in a Brigham Young University Studies journal in 1977. The footnote describes this outrageous fakery, **The Mormon Heritage of Vardis Fisher**, as a "revisionist article that corrects earlier assumptions." The only "earlier assumption" this "revisionist article" "corrects" is any assumption anybody might ever have entertained that a Church Historian for the Church of Jesus Christ of Latter Day Saints must be a man who has a high regard for the Ten Commandments, and a thorough grounding in proper procedures for scholarly research.

In a book to be published early next winter, entitled: **...False Witness,** I shall offer a fully documented exposé of this ghoulish attempt by the Mormons to claim as their own — now that he is dead and defenseless — a man whom they alternately vilified and courted for years, *but never dared to claim while he lived*. Fisher never made any secret of the fact that he had nothing but contempt for the Mormon hierarchy, the Mormon "religion" (which in his opinion was not *religion* at all), and for the Mormon way of life, which he considered stultifying in the extreme.

Nobody needs to take my word for anything: Vardis will speak for himself in my book, beginning with sonnets from his first published work, **Sonnets to an Imaginary Madonna** (1927), to his scholarly **Testament of Man Series.** There will be quotations from interviews and articles; from personal letters; and statements or letters from persons who knew Vardis all those years.

Here is an example of what I'm talking about: In 1942, on page 459 of **Twentieth Century Authors**, edited by Stanley J. Kunitz and Howard Haycroft (New York: H.W. Wilson), Fisher was quoted: "I have one brother, Dr. V.E. Fisher, a psychologist, and an atheist like myself; and a sister, Irene, who is pious enough for a whole tribe." In their dishonest article, Arrington and Haupt have perverted Fisher's contemptuous dismissal of his sister to their own ends as follows: Leaving out the first part of the quotation altogether, they say: "There is a touch of pleasure and need in Vardis' characterization of his sister as 'pious enough for a whole tribe,'[5] as though he were counting on her to arrange that his temple work be done for him after he died (which of course she did)." (Footnote 5 cites **Twentieth Century Authors** as the inspiration for this pious, hypocritical drivel!)

In the paragraph following the above quotation (page 28, B.Y.U. Studies, Fall issue, 1977), the authors say: "Fisher was not an apostate; he never renounced his religion..." If it's true that these men actually read Fisher's tetralogy, as Arrington assured me they had, they knew this was a lie when they wrote it. In the third volume (**We Are Betrayed**, 1935), page 34, Fisher, as Vridar, says unequivocally: "I am not a Christian." On page 255 in this book (he is still a student at the University of Chicago) he says: "Vridar now definitely renounced all orthodox religions; because they all sprang, it seemed to him, from guilt and vanity and fear." On pages 247-248, Vridar not only renounces Mormonism, but denounces it, when two young Mormon missionaries appear at his door and declare that they have been sent to reclaim him for the Church. He amuses himself by baiting them for an hour or so, until one of them finally says: "Then you don't want a-be a Mormon any more?" And Vridar answers coldly, "Of course not. It's the silliest of all the Protestant religions.''

Fisher's last important interview was videotaped at the University of South Dakota, in 1967. In it, he said flatly that he was not a Mormon. Dr. John Milton then asked: ''Are there problems in your family? Do they resent the fact that you have left the Mormon Church?'' Fisher's mocking, ironic reply: ''Oh, yes. I suppose. Those closest to me have resented it.'' (Milton chuckles.) ''And there's my sister! My dear, devout, devoted sister (said derisively) — is *still* doing her best to save my soul.'' (Milton is amused.) ''But, uh . . . Some persons who read **My Holy Satan** in my **Testament of Man** series of novels, are now trying to save my soul also, because *they* are devout Catholics. So, now I have both Catholics and Mormons trying to save me, and I think my chances must be pretty good!''

Open Letter to:
Spencer W. Kimball, President
Church of Jesus Christ of Latter-Day Saints

Dear Sir:

Having read the press release, you know that I am going to expose the fraudulent, hypocritical article published in a Brigham Young University Studies Journal in 1977, by Leonard J. Arrington, Mormon Church Historian.

In addition to the book I am compiling to set the record straight, I shall also see to it that there is a page of biographical data in every Fisher book that comes off the press from now on. Yes, even after I'm dead; even after the copyrights have expired. And I've set up a fund to be sure that the books will be in print in perpetuity. These biographical data sheets will make it clear, for the guidance of future researchers, that the Arrington/Haupt article is a lie.

That's what *I'm* going to do about it.

Now. The question is: What are *you* going to do about it?

What are you, as President, Prophet, Seer and Revelator of the Church of Jesus Christ of Latter-day Saints, going to do about it?

Are you going to do the only honorable thing possible? — admit to the world at large, and to those trusting students at B.Y.U., who were deliberately deceived, that VARDIS FISHER WAS NOT A MORMON; did not have a Mormon indoctrination during his formative years in the home of his father; that he had apostatized from the Mormon Church within a year after his baptism, without ever having followed through on anything that would

81

have qualified him as a Mormon? Are you going to remove this crass and stupid forgery from the Mormon archives? Are you going to instruct B.Y.U. Press to destroy any copies it has on hand, and make sure that this Church-owned school never again publishes such a lie about Vardis Fisher?

Or are you, by remaining silent, by doing nothing, going to put your God in the position of supporting the pious, hypocritical lie published by your official Church Historian?

Over four millions (it is said) of Latter-day Saints look to you as God's representative on earth, and believe that God speaks to them through you. There are, then, over four millions of naïve, credulous faces of the faithful turned towards you always; and, on occasion, beyond them, there are millions of faces of the skeptics looking at you with tolerant amusement, with smirks of contempt, with leers and jeers, or with purely clinical interest, to see what you will do when your Church is called to account.

Judging from your past performance, I haven't the slightest notion of what you will do this time; but I take my position among those who will watch with clinical interest, curious to observe the psychological reaction of a cult leader, when he is faced with the fact that there are still persons around who are not to be intimidated, either by superstitious dread, or by the wrath of an extremely wealthy and powerful and ruthless and well-established church.

I am one of them,
Opal Laurel Holmes
(Mrs. Vardis Fisher)

To the EDITORS:

BIOGRAPHICAL DATA: Vardis Fisher was born March 31, 1895; died July 9, 1968; B.A. University of Utah, 1920; M.A. University of Chicago, 1922; Ph.D. (magna cum laude) from the University of Chicago. He was a Phi Beta Kappa. Married three times: Leona McMurtrey (two sons: Grant and Wayne), 1917; suicide 1924; married Margaret Trusler, 1928 (one son: Thornton Roberts); divorce 1939; married Opal Laurel Holmes, 1940 (no children).

"...Fisher had three reputations — as a writer of regional and naturalistic novels in the late twenties and early thirties [**Dark Bridwell, In Tragic Life**]...as a writer of historical novels with a western setting]**Tale of Valor** (Lewis and Clark), **The Mothers** (Donner party), **City of Illusion** (Comstock Lode)]...as a writer of historical novels with a powerful and controversial evolutionary thesis (his **Testament of Man Series**)." This is taken from an introduction to a bibliography by George Kellogg, Ph.D., Humanities Librarian, University of Idaho.

"The methodology which Fisher employed in writing the historical novel lends itself to being criticized with the same techniques as those used in history...can be criticized with the same strictures because it is constructed by methods similar to those used by historians... [Fisher insisted] that a broad social science approach to gathering historical evidence is necessary... he created a new concept of fiction and a new task for the historical novelist..." Ronald W. Taber, Ph.D., Literary Historian.

A Word to the Reader

I very much regret having to put this unpleasant material into all of Fisher's books, but when one lone citizen is fighting (at Fisher's expressed wish) an organization as rich and powerful, as ruthless and relentlessly vindictive, as determined to prevail, as the Mormon leaders, one must use any means at hand that may prove effective.

Surely these sonnets say, as clearly as any man ever said it, that Fisher was an "unbeliever" (see sonnets forty-three through forty-nine and the one on page fifty-eight) — an atheist.

He had, in 1916, after one incredulous reading of the Mormon "holy books," following an impulsive baptism, cast the "stupid, primitive stuff" out of his life, in the spirit in which one tosses a piece of worthless paper into a wastebasket; and never again gave it serious consideration except as a motivating factor in a fascinating episode of American history. That was eleven years before **Sonnets to an Imaginary Madonna** was published, and twenty-three years before **Children of God**, an American historical novel, was published.

I read a paper on this subject (Arrington's lies about Vardis Fisher) to a small group, and after it was over, a Mormon woman introduced herself and said, with heavy sarcasm: "You say Dr. Arrington didn't properly research the article in the B.Y.U. journal — I'd like to point out to you, that *Doctor* Arrington earned a Ph.D. — *that* ought to prove something!"

It certainly does! It proves that you can lead a donkey to logic, but you can't make him think.